CAREERS IN
UNDERCOVER GANG
INVESTIGATION

CAREERS IN

UNDERCOVER GANG INVESTIGATION

JASON PORTERFIELD

ROSEN
PUBLISHING®

New York

Published in 2014 by The Rosen Publishing Group, Inc.
29 East 21st Street, New York, NY 10010

First Edition

Library of Congress Cataloging-in-Publication Data

Porterfield, Jason.
Careers in undercover gang investigation/Jason Porterfield.
    pages cm.—(Extreme law enforcement)
Includes bibliographical references and index.
ISBN 978-1-4777-1712-7 (library binding)
1. Undercover operations—United States—Juvenile literature.
2. Gangs—United States—Juvenile literature. 3. Law enforcement—Vocational guidance—United States—Juvenile literature. I. Title.
HV8080.U5P67 2014
363.25—dc23

                                                                2013011012

Manufactured in the United States of America

CPSIA Compliance Information: Batch #W14YA: For further information, contact Rosen Publishing, New York, New York, at 1-800-237-9932.

CONTENTS

INTRODUCTION

Criminal gangs are among the most persistent public safety problems in the United States. Some gangs are highly sophisticated organizations with thousands of members and cover large geographic areas. Others may consist of just a few people and cover only a block or two. They may be street gangs, outlaw motorcycle gangs, or prison gangs.

A recent study by the Federal Bureau of Investigation (FBI) found there are about 33,000 street gangs, outlaw motorcycle gangs, and prison gangs in the United States, with an estimated total membership of about 1.4 million. Alarmingly, this number represents a dramatic jump from the previous total gang membership of about one million recorded in 2009.

In order to crack down on gangs, law enforcement agencies sometimes use undercover gang investigators to gather information about a gang's suspected criminal activities. Careers for undercover gang investigators are available in local and state police departments, as well as several federal law enforcement agencies, including the FBI.

These officers and agents have one of the most challenging jobs in law enforcement. They have to pose as gang members and gain the trust of the gang that they are investigating. Most importantly they have to gather information

An undercover gang investigator displays a badge identifying him as a member of the Orange County (California) Sheriff's Department. In order to do their jobs, undercover investigators must keep their identities concealed.

about the gang without being discovered. The work often keeps them away from their families and friends and may place enormous pressure on them.

Undercover gang investigators live with the constant threat of being found out, injured, or even killed. They have to stay calm when they see gang members commit crimes. They

7

may even have to participate in criminal acts themselves in order to maintain their cover. While they are undercover, they stay in contact with an investigative team that stands by to provide protection and support for the investigator. At the conclusion of a successful undercover investigation, the evidence gathered may lead to criminal charges, convictions, and jail time for gang members.

Work as an undercover gang investigator is not for everyone. However, resourceful law enforcement officers and agents with a strong sense of integrity, the ability to act out a role, and the inner strength to deal with enormous pressure can turn undercover work into a rewarding career.

CHAPTER ONE

THE TEAM BEHIND AN UNDERCOVER GANG INVESTIGATION

When a group of four alleged gang members in Illinois decided to rob a house in Chicago that they thought contained narcotics, they carefully planned the crime. According to a *Chicago Tribune* article, the men stashed weapons in their car and checked each other for hidden listening devices to make sure that no one in the group was an undercover officer. Convinced that the police weren't watching, they prepared to go ahead with the robbery.

However, it turned out that one of the men involved in the planning had been working undercover with federal investigators, and police had been informed of the planned robbery. Despite the checks for recording devices, investigators had managed to record much of the group's prior planning. The men were arrested and charged with intent to distribute narcotics.

The arrests were part of a two-year investigation of the Latin Kings street gang. Investigators targeted the gang's narcotics distribution network, resulting in federal narcotics charges against twenty-six alleged gang members, leaders,

Gang graffiti marks an intersection near the site of a fatal shooting in Chicago, Illinois. Gangs sometimes take control of blocks or even entire neighborhoods, often intimidating or pushing out law-abiding citizens.

and associates. A federal agent working undercover was able to work his way into several factions within the gang and gain the trust of gang leaders.

Police Gang Units at Work

The investigator who went undercover to apprehend the suspected Chicago gang members, the agents and officers providing backup, and the technicians who helped collect and analyze the evidence against them were all doing highly specialized work as part of a gang unit.

Police gang units are made up of officers and detectives who have been trained to investigate gangs and the crimes they commit. During their investigations, they may

COERCION IN UNDERCOVER INVESTIGATIONS

Coercion is the act of trapping, tricking, or pressuring a person into committing a criminal act. The people who are arrested at the end of an undercover investigation often accuse the police department of coercion. When suspects are successful in proving that they were coerced into committing a crime, they seriously damage the district attorney's case. They may even get the charges against them dismissed.

Officers are trained to avoid pushing suspects into illegal behavior. Undercover investigators in particular must be careful to avoid rushing suspects into breaking the law because they carry so much responsibility for gathering good evidence that will hold up in court. Surveillance recordings are often used to show that undercover officers did not coerce suspects. If officers can show that the suspect was merely given the opportunity to commit a crime and could have walked away at any time without doing anything illegal, the court is more likely to side with the police.

work with a variety of specialized technicians to gather information. They may also work with outside experts, such as community leaders and criminologists, to put together a complete picture of a gang's activities.

These investigations may take months or years to complete. However, the investigators often uncover many facets of the operations of large criminal organizations. If an investigation goes well, the information gathered can be used to prosecute gang members and their leaders for the crimes they committed during the course of the investigation. They can even be charged with older crimes if the investigators can gather the necessary evidence.

Technology and advances in evidence-gathering techniques can make it easier than it once was to build a case against an alleged gang member who is linked to a crime scene. However, police departments still often need someone who can get inside the gang and gather firsthand insider information in order to catch others who were involved in the crime or who took part in related crimes.

Bringing in an Undercover Investigator

There are times when police departments suspect that criminal activity is taking place but they have no proof of a crime. They may have only heard rumors or received an anonymous tip about the criminal activity. This is particularly true in the case of gang activity. Gang members who are caught

Undercover gang investigators in Buena Park, California, interview white supremacist gang members while investigating a possible stolen vehicle. Such interviews can help investigators learn about how a gang operates.

committing a crime often are not willing to talk about the gang's activities or reveal the identities of other members of the gang. While police may be able to bring charges against individual gang members, it may be difficult for them to use the evidence available to prove that a larger criminal organization is at work. The department may need to infiltrate the gang in order to gather the necessary evidence.

Undercover gang investigators fill this role as part of these special investigative units. They take on a role that allows them to work their way into a gang's culture. They may pose as low-level criminals in order to become part of a gang. Once they have established themselves as part of the gang and gain the trust of gang members, they can learn details about how the gang works and the crimes that its members commit.

Most police officers are capable of working undercover in at least some limited situations. Some officers are drawn to the work, while others are repelled by it. Being an undercover gang investigator is stressful and dangerous. The investigator must find a way to fit into the gang's culture while trying to avoid actually committing crimes. He or she must be able to speak the gang's language, learn and use its signs correctly, and be able to identify rivals.

The undercover investigator may be asked to participate in crimes. Many departments have particular rules about what criminal acts an undercover officer is allowed to commit in order to maintain cover. In such cases, he or she would likely have to seek permission from the investigation's supervisor before proceeding.

A Hidden Force

Undercover gang investigators undergo the same training as other police officers. They are trained in police academies and go to

A police officer uses a video simulator to practice following a suspect at a police training academy in Nokesville, Virginia.

work in local law enforcement departments, or they get jobs with a county sheriff's office or a state police department. No matter where they are employed, all new officers spend a set number of years on patrol at the beginning of their career. During this time, they are watched by their fellow officers and superiors, who note their strengths and weaknesses.

Police officers who have a particular interest in becoming undercover gang investigators may spend five or six years taking special courses on how to carry out undercover work. They work hard to learn as much as they can about under-cover techniques and about the gangs they want to infiltrate. They show their interest by working hard at their police job. Many successful undercover gang investigators show an ability to interact easily with gang members early in their policing career. Above all, they have to show that they can put in the long hours and extreme effort that it takes to carry out undercover work.

Officers who demonstrate a talent for the work and put in the time may be assigned to work with undercover gang investigators. They learn from these veteran officers before they get to go out in the field themselves. At first, they may be assigned to smaller undercover roles in shorter investigations or to supporting roles within a larger investi-gation. These junior investigators may work to help establish the main undercover investigator's credibility through interactions with him or her that appear to be criminal, such as faking a fight or a robbery, or purchasing narcotics or weapons. The experience they gain in these small roles can help them gain confidence before taking on larger roles.

Technicians and Analysts

Antigang units rely on other police personnel to help them gather the information they need to make a case against gang members. Police technicians are often vital to undercover gang investigations. Many larger police departments have technicians who specialize in setting up and operating remote surveillance equipment. This can include cameras, recording devices, hidden microphones, wiretaps, and transmitters to gather information. Technicians may also help officers with remote surveillance in disguised vehicles or in covert locations, such as houses or storefronts located near a gang's headquarters.

Evidence technicians gather evidence from crime scenes to help officers and detectives figure out what happened. They gather evidence from many sorts of crimes. They may not be assigned specifically to assist in an undercover gang investigation. However, the officers carrying out the investigation may ask them for information on previous cases or on current crimes in which the people they are investigating are suspects.

Equipment technicians help set up and maintain electronics and surveillance equipment. Undercover gang

Some police officers and personnel work behind the scenes to provide support to officers in the field. Here, an officer monitors equipment that pinpoints locations where gunshots were fired.

investigators often use sophisticated surveillance equipment to record the actions of the gang members they are investigating. This equipment may include high-tech microphones, audio recorders, video and still cameras, and devices designed to intercept telephone signals or other means of electronic communication. These surveillance devices can be so small that they can easily be concealed, either on the undercover investigator's body or belongings or near a spot where conversations can be overheard.

Intelligence analysts interpret data gathered during an investigation. The information is examined for evidence of criminal activities. The information is also crucial for keeping undercover investigators informed of evidence that points to changes in how the gang operates. Information gathered and interpreted by these analysts can help gang investigators create and refine their undercover personas.

The District Attorney

The district attorney, also referred to as the prosecutor, is the person who brings charges against accused criminals, called defendants, and argues the cases against them in court. The district attorney's job is to represent the government and the law in criminal proceedings against accused lawbreakers. Prosecutors work on municipal, county, state, and federal levels. In some larger jurisdictions, prosecutors may

Confiscated drugs and money are displayed as U.S. attorney Carmen Ortiz announces the arrest of thirty gang members for drug and firearms offenses in Boston, Massachusetts.

specialize in one particular area of the law. In smaller jurisdictions, a single prosecutor may argue all criminal cases. Prosecutors may be elected or appointed to their posts.

Being a prosecutor is a very powerful position and comes with a great deal of responsibility. Prosecutors have to use their judgment in deciding whether a defendant should be charged and which charges should be brought against him or her. The prosecutor is present for the bail hearing, presents evidence before grand juries, carries out investigations, interviews witnesses, appears at pre- and post-trial hearings, and writes legal opinions.

When a case goes to trial, the prosecutor must prove that the accused is guilty beyond a reasonable doubt. The judge or jury presiding over the case must weigh and consider the prosecutor's evidence against the competing evidence presented by defense attorneys. The judge or jury then decide whether or not to convict the defendant.

Prosecutors and law enforcement work together to prepare a case. The prosecutor issues warrants and gauges if there is enough evidence to press charges. If not, the prosecutor may have the police investigate further to gather more conclusive evidence.

People often see prosecutors as trial lawyers who are determined to convict a suspect, but this perception of their role is skewed. The prosecutor's job is to serve justice, rather than simply winning convictions. If a prosecutor uncovers evidence during an investigation that could help the defense and clear someone who is wrongfully accused, he or she must turn it over to the defendant. Many criminal cases are resolved by plea bargaining between the prosecutor and defendant and never even go to trial.

Prosecutors encounter gang members who are accused of many kinds of offenses, ranging from misdemeanor crimes, such as simple battery or vandalism, to felony drug or weapons charges or even murder. In undercover gang investigations, the district attorney's office decides if enough evidence has been gathered to make arrests and then uses that evidence to try to convict gang members. Often prosecutors will try to use evidence against individuals to get them to reveal more information about other suspects or about the gang's operations. In exchange for cooperation, the prosecutor may reduce the charges or ask for a more lenient sentence for the accused gang member.

Many people apart from the prosecutor play roles in a district attorney's office. They include paralegals, law clerks, researchers, legal assistants, and assistant or deputy prosecutors.

Civilian Positions

Most police departments employ civilians in support roles. Forensic technicians and crime lab scientists are civilians, for example. They are not police officers. In carrying out their duties, civilian employees work alongside sworn police officers. Civilians fill many of a department's technical and administrative positions.

Dispatchers are responsible for taking phone calls from the public requesting assistance from the police with emergency and nonemergency situations. The dispatchers must determine the nature of the situation and send out the appropriate unit to respond to the call. They need to be able to coax important information from the caller, such as a location and whether anyone is in immediate danger.

Civilians may also oversee a police department's payrolls, budgets, computer systems, personnel, facilities, and equipment. They perform many of the administrative duties that help the department run smoothly. They may staff the front desks and take care of police records and reports. Administrative staff members assist police officers and deal with the general public. Public relations personnel help the police department keep the public informed and educated on public safety issues. In addition, many gang investigations units have an administrative assistant to help keep up with the paperwork.

CHAPTER TWO

INFILTRATING A GANG

I n July 2012, residents of the small town of Holland, Michigan, learned that four men had been arrested for alleged crimes connected with the Latin Kings street gang. The gang had been present in the town for about two decades. In the months leading up to the arrests, however, there had been an increase in low-level gang activity, such as reports of graffiti and street fights. The investigation into the gang began on a small scale about twenty years before the arrests were made. But it gained momentum in 2010, when local law enforcement joined forces with federal agencies including the FBI and the Drug Enforcement Administration (DEA).

The arrests were the result of a more intensive, yearlong investigation of the Latin Kings. Local and state police worked with federal agencies to gather evidence. The investigation included conducting undercover surveillance of informants making drug purchases from members of the gang. The four initial arrests turned into a bigger success story as more information about the gang's activities came to light. Investigators were ultimately able to gather enough information about other suspected gang members to indict thirty-one members of the Latin Kings on charges ranging from racketeering and conspiracy to distribute narcotics to weapons violations.

The arrests would not have been possible without undercover gang investigators who were able to get close enough to gang members to gather crucial evidence. Investigators discovered and collected evidence of a far-reaching criminal organization that included a network for moving narcotics and guns that spanned several states. The gang also allegedly used its own system of background checks to keep track of informants who might be moving from state to state. Undercover gang investigators were able to carry out surveillance of the gang's activities and make secret recordings of gang meetings. Their success in the lengthy investigation highlights the challenges that undercover gang investigators often face when going up against a highly organized gang.

Los Angeles Police Department gang unit officers search a group of men who had been caught drinking in public in an area controlled by the Grape Street Crips street gang.

The Spread of Gangs

Gangs have long been assumed to be a problem only in urban areas. Their presence and the crimes they commit are indeed a persistent problem in many cities. Yet gangs also cause problems in suburbs and small towns. Gang operations may even move out into rural areas, as gang leaders look for ways to avoid police interference in their activities.

Gangs are most often defined by law enforcement as organizations that take part in criminal, threatening, or intimidating behavior within a community. These groups consist of three or more individuals, and they evolve and grow within their community. They have a recognized leadership structure and often create a code of conduct for members to follow. The gang stays together during periods of peace and in times of conflict with rivals. Gang members often hold regular meetings. Belonging to a gang gives its members a shared sense of identity, which they may express through symbols, hand signs, wearing certain colors, graffiti, and even tattoos. They compete with other gangs for territory and rely on violence and intimidation to hold onto it.

The crimes committed by gang members can cover a broad range of actions, from assaults against rival gang members, vandalism, and the manufacturing and selling of narcotics to thefts, robberies, arson, and fraud. Gangs work to carve out a particular area, or "turf," where they can carry out their criminal activities without interference from or competition with other gangs. They resort to violence and intimidation in order to scare law-abiding residents from taking action to support police efforts.

Types of Gangs

When most people think of gangs, they think of urban street gangs. Street gangs are probably the most common gangs in the United States. They can be found throughout the country, and they vary greatly in size, ethnic makeup, composition, and structure. Some street gangs have a national presence and engage in large-scale criminal operations. These can include smuggling, producing, transporting, and distributing illegal narcotics throughout the country. These gangs can be extremely violent as they protect their interests. Gangs with a national reach include the Latin Kings, the Crips, the Bloods, Mara Salvatrucha (sometimes called MS-13), and the Vice Lords.

Smaller street gangs in urban, suburban, and rural areas engage in many of the same practices as their larger counterparts, though their activities are limited to a much smaller territory and are on a far smaller scale. They often imitate the worst, most violent excesses of the larger gangs in order to gain respect from local rivals. The Justice Department considers larger gangs to be the greatest threat to public safety, but even small gangs create significant problems for law enforcement agencies.

Outlaw motorcycle gangs are criminal organizations that evolved from legal and legitimate motorcycle clubs. These

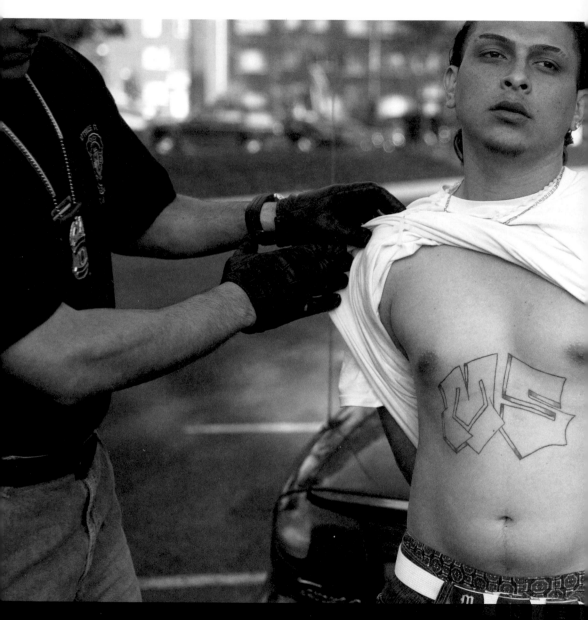

Antigang officers in Maryland take a member of the Mara Salvatrucha street gang into custody. The suspect's tattoos, belt, and clothing mark him as a member of the gang.

gangs now use their motorcycle clubs to carry out criminal activity, including violent crime, drug trafficking, and weapons trafficking. More than three hundred outlaw motorcycle gangs operate within the United States, ranging in size from a single chapter with five or six members to international organizations with thousands of members and chapters around the world. Large motorcycle gangs classified as outlaws by the Justice Department include the Hells Angels, Bandidos, Outlaws, and Sons of Silence. According to the Justice Department, these four gangs are responsible for most of the crimes linked to outlaw motorcycle gangs, particularly smuggling drugs into the United States from other countries.

Members of the Outlaws motorcycle gang ride to the funeral of a fellow gang member who died during a shoot-out with ATF agents who were trying to arrest him.

Prison gangs are gangs that first formed in jails and now operate throughout the U.S. penal system, as well as outside correctional facilities. Prison gangs are organized, with a distinct hierarchy and a code of conduct for members to follow. Some of these gangs have organizations that span many prisons throughout the United States. Most are organized along racial or ethnic lines and are extremely violent. Inmates often join prison gangs as a way to gain protection from other prisoners. Inside prisons, these gangs may smuggle drugs and other contraband items, carry out beatings or murders for hire, or protect other prisoners in exchange for money or other valuables. Joining gangs is generally against prison rules, but many prison gang members do not take the threat of punishment seriously.

Prison gangs extend their reach to the outside world when members finish serving their sentences and are released. Gang members who are released and refuse to take part in criminal activity may be threatened, hurt, or even killed if they return to prison. Outside the prison system, these gangs often function as links between criminal organizations that smuggle drugs and street gangs or outlaw motorcycle gangs. The Mexican Mafia and Aryan Brotherhood are among the most notorious prison gangs.

Keeping Up with Gangs

Police departments often keep files on gangs and any gang members that have been identified, usually through arrests. Officers make note of whether an arrestee is wearing an identifying piece of clothing, has a tattoo, or was seen displaying gang signs or heard uttering gang slogans. Witnesses may identify a suspect as a gang member, and gang members sometimes identify themselves as such to police.

Even the most diligent police force can only scratch the surface in terms of identifying gang members. Gangs are fluid organizations. Small gangs may form and disband even before a police force becomes aware of them. Members may drop out of the gang, shift their allegiances to other gangs, move away, or wind up in jail.

Some gang members are proud to display their gang colors, use gang slogans in public, and draw attention to their gang affiliation in other ways. These gang members often attract police attention. Officers may stop them for questioning, even when they aren't committing a crime. They may take gang members into custody if they can find even a flimsy reason for doing so.

Other gang members keep a lower profile in order to avoid police attention. They want to stay free so that they can continue committing crimes without being bothered by the police. These gang members keep their gang affiliations under wraps and are subtler about how they identify themselves to other people. Police officers may even arrest these gang members and charge them with crimes unrelated to gang activity without ever knowing or realizing that they belong to a gang.

Starting an Investigation

When gang members are arrested, police officers often try to get them to identify other members of their gang or talk about gang activities. With the backing of the local prosecutor, they may offer leniency to a gang member who gives them good information that they can use to build an investigation. Or they might threaten harsh sentences for withholding information.

Some gang members willingly give officers information. They may be tired of being in a gang or acting in retaliation for some slight committed against them by other gang members. Higher-level gang members may give police information on rivals or other gang members whom they see as a threat to their position in the gang. They may feel that they have enough supporters in the gang to ensure that the members they inform on can't hurt them.

Other gang members refuse to talk to the police about gang activities. They may see talking to police officers as an act of betrayal against their fellow gang members. They may be afraid that if they do talk to the police, other gang members will seek revenge against them. Their gangs may reward them for keeping silent, which increases their standing in the gang once they are released from jail.

Investigators look into every aspect of a jailed gang member's life. They talk to relatives, neighbors, and associates in order to gather information. Armed with search warrants, they examine the gang member's home, property, computers and digital and mobile devices, phone records, and personal records to build a case for prosecutors.

Often an undercover gang investigation starts with rumors that officers hear of local gang activity. Members of the community may tell officers about new graffiti appearing in a neighborhood or some other suspicious activity that could signal that a gang has started moving in or intensified their activities. Officers look for patterns in terms of the kinds of stops and arrests that they make in an area. If they notice an increase in gang activity or the presence of a new gang in an area, they may make a note of it in their reports. As information comes together through police activity and witness reports, gang investigators may decide that the time has come to begin an undercover investigation.

Setting Up an Investigation

Every undercover gang investigation starts with gathering information

A Chicago Police Department narcotics officer works undercover to gather information against suspected drug dealers. In order to do such work, undercover officers must be patient and observant.

about a gang based on crime reports, rumors, or statements by informants. Investigators start out by mapping the gang's territory and putting together information on its activities, its known members, and any rivals or allies. This preliminary part of the investigation may last for weeks as investigators familiarize themselves with the gang's operations and territory.

Once the investigative team is familiar with the gang, a role is developed for the undercover officer to play. Undercover gang investigators are usually allowed to come up with their own cover stories. They have to be convincing in order to gain the gang's trust, so they may use information that they have gleaned from old cases or informants as raw material for their cover stories. As the investigation advances, they may enlist the help of government agencies in putting together phony documents to help support their story. The investigator starts working on developing the mind-set of a gang member and creating a "look" to use during a case. He or she will need to get clothing, jewelry, and accessories that will be in keeping with the way that the members of that particular gang look, dress, and act.

Getting Inside

Once the undercover investigator is ready, he or she has to find a way to be introduced to the gang. Gangs are insular and secretive groups. While gangs are always looking to expand, members are often cautious around outsiders they don't know.

They may become suspicious if a new person they have not encountered before starts coming around, looking to join.

Gang investigators often use informants to help an undercover investigator get into a gang. One common strategy is for the informant to introduce the undercover investigator as a friend, relative, or acquaintance. The informant and the investigator may hang out together with gang members while the investigator gains the gang's trust and then distance themselves from each other. The undercover investigator may then bring in another undercover investigator as a friend. The first undercover investigator then gradually drops out of the gang while the new investigator gains the gang's trust. This tactic separates the investigator who is actually going to be undercover most of the time from the informant and lessens the danger of the informant revealing the undercover investigator's identity.

Working the Case

Undercover investigators usually start their investigation by gathering evidence about low-level gang members. Then they work their way up to members of higher stature or in leadership positions. During the operation, the investigative team will work out a system in which the undercover investigator can turn evidence over to the other, non-undercover investigators.

The undercover investigator is supervised as closely as possible during the investigation. When possible, other members of the team will be watching their undercover counterpart. Investigative teams have many ways to do this. They may establish other "characters" in the neighborhood where the investigation is taking place, putting more disguised investigators in the same vicinity as the primary undercover investigator. Other officers and technicians may be posted in surveillance vehicles—often vans or panel trucks that have been disguised—or in a temporary staging ground located in a nearby house or storefront. From these locations, other members of the investigative team can observe the proceedings and make recordings that can later be used as evidence.

Undercover investigators working to establish trust among the gang members may have to prove their loyalty or their criminality. They may do this by staging a showdown with regular police officers or some other brush with the law in which it appears that they have committed a crime. Many undercover investigations include staged arrests of undercover officers. These "arrests" give the rest of the investigative team a chance to check up on the officer and for the undercover officer to give a report of how the investigation is going.

The investigation's supervisor or a prosecutor will make the decision about whether enough evidence has been gathered to bring charges against enough major or mid-level gang members to end the operation. If the operation becomes too risky for the undercover investigator, it may be brought to an end before a case can be made against the highest-ranking

ANXIETY LINGERS LONG AFTER THE CASE IS CLOSED

The family lives of undercover investigators often suffer during and long after an undercover gang assignment. Many police officers worry about the possibility of a criminal finding out who they are and seeking revenge against their family members. For most, the possibility is very remote. Undercover investigators, however, have to immerse themselves in a gang culture that values loyalty and harshly punishes disloyalty. They may have witnessed harsh reprisals against rival gang members over the course of an investigation lasting weeks, months, or even years. Even after an investigation is over, undercover officers may worry about being discovered and pursued by the people they helped arrest.

members of the gang. Instead, prosecutors bring charges in the cases in which they have enough evidence to obtain a conviction, even if it is only against lower-level members.

Riding Out an Investigation

The safety of the undercover investigator is always more important than the results of a given investigation. The investigative team and prosecutors will continue to emphasize this to the undercover officer throughout an investigation. They will remind the undercover officer or agent that he or she has the support of the unit. They will emphasize the importance of halting the investigation if there is any danger of the undercover investigator being exposed or hurt.

Carrying out a lengthy undercover investigation can be draining. The undercover officer must fully enter the gang life. He or she may be asked to do things that are illegal, dangerous, or against his or her nature. Gang members may involve the undercover officer in dangerous situations. Many undercover officers find ways to avoid getting involved in any crimes that are committed by gang members. They may fake an illness or injury or arrange to be "arrested" by other officers in order to come up with a believable excuse for the avoidance of criminal activity.

Long-running investigations place tremendous stress on undercover investigators. During the course of the investigation, the undercover investigator may make friends with gang members. He or she may start to question the purpose of the investigation or perhaps be tempted to share in the gang's illegal activities. If the undercover investigator has to go for a long period of time without contact from the rest of the investigative team, he or she may feel abandoned by the other members of the team.

Some undercover investigators have reported that after a while they begin to feel paranoid that the gang members

A gang unit detective searches the apartment of a suspected drug dealer in Los Angeles while carrying out a search warrant. Officers recovered drugs, guns, and cash from the scene.

know that they are working undercover. They may also come to believe that the officers they are working with suspect them of engaging in actual illegal activity. This paranoia can put the investigation at risk and place the lives of those involved in danger. An investigation may be cut short if an undercover investigator becomes too paranoid to continue with the operation.

Concluding the Investigation

Once the prosecutor feels confident that he or she has enough evidence to bring charges against gang members, the team starts wrapping up the investigation. They obtain arrest and search warrants from a judge and make arrests, seizing any evidence they are authorized to take. Patrol officers and sometimes Special Weapons and Tactics (SWAT) officers are brought in to help make the arrests. Extracting the undercover officer often involves "arresting" him or her shortly before police arrest the real suspects, though sometimes the undercover investigator is "arrested" along with the real gang members. In other cases, the undercover investigator may gradually fade out of the gang life. He or she may also abruptly leave town after offering a cover story to other gang members. Officers later do everything they can to erase any trace of the undercover officer's identity and protect his or her anonymity.

After the initial arrests are made, detectives often use interrogation tactics to try to get gang members to reveal information that could lead to more arrests. Prosecutors may allow detectives to offer a plea deal to gang members who cooperate. Detectives may also threaten reluctant gang members with long jail sentences. During long and grueling interrogation sessions, even gang members who are reluctant to talk to detectives may let information slip that could lead to more arrests.

CHAPTER THREE

THE SKILLS NEEDED TO GO UNDERCOVER AND STAY UNDERCOVER

I t takes a special kind of resilience to be a full-time undercover gang investigator. Undercover gang investigators stay undercover in the field for weeks, months, or even years. They have to keep up their role at all times, and they have to make it believable. Many gang members, particularly gang leaders, are suspicious of nearly everyone around them, including those compatriots who have been with them for years. Any hint that the undercover gang investigator is not what he or she appears to be can compromise the entire operation. Even worse, it could put the undercover investigator and other members of the investigative team in danger.

Experience Is Key

Training in law enforcement is vital for an undercover gang investigator. Undercover gang investigators tend to be younger officers or officers with a youthful appearance. This helps them blend in with real gang members, who are often in their teens or early twenties. It is some-what rare for officers to begin their careers by working on undercover assignments. Many police departments prefer that officers gain experience patrolling a beat. This allows superiors to gauge how an officer works and inter-acts with people encountered on the street. An officer who can talk and behave with confidence and ease around a wide cross-section of people may be seen as a perfect candidate for under-cover work. It helps if he or she is approachable.

Some undercover investigators spend years honing their investigative skills before taking on an undercover role. In other cases, officers may be selected for undercover work right out of the police academy. Departments who choose fresh recruits for undercover work may be looking for officers with a particular look or specific language skills. Fresh recruits are also less likely to be known on the street by gang members.

Many undercover skills can be learned. Undercover investigators can study gang behavior and identifiers such

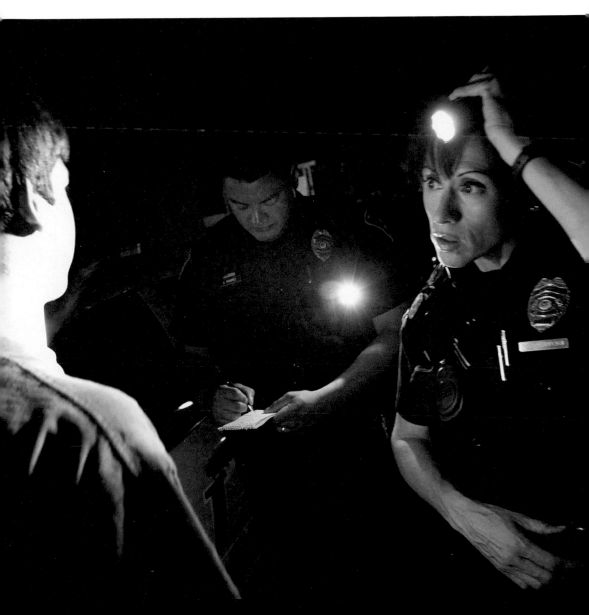

Officers learn how to interact with many different kinds of people and deal with a variety of situations by working a beat. Here, an officer interviews a young assault victim.

WILLIAM QUEEN

In 1998, Bureau of Alcohol, Tobacco, Firearms, and Explosives (ATF) agent William Queen was given the task of infiltrating the Mongols motorcycle gang in California's San Fernando Valley. Queen was a motorcycle enthusiast, and his superiors at the agency picked him as the best candidate to take on the role of a long-haired, bearded biker gang member.

During the two-year undercover investigation, Queen succeeded in becoming a full member of the gang, rising to the rank of treasurer. His undercover work ultimately led to the arrest of fifty-four gang members, fifty-three of whom were later convicted of charges including drug trafficking and conspiracy to commit murder.

During the investigation, Queen was completely cut off from his family and colleagues. He often had to prove himself to gang members by taking part in crimes, including drug and weapons trafficking and stealing motorcycles. Queen later described the sense of isolation and the camaraderie he sometimes felt with gang members in his memoir, *Undercover and Alone* (2005).

as gang colors, slogans, and signs. They can learn the language of the street and how to interact with suspected criminals on a daily basis without arousing suspicion. Their police training teaches them how to use their powers of observation and how to assess a dangerous situation.

The whole investigative team, particularly the undercover investigator, must be disciplined and able to follow instructions. Complex undercover investigations often include long planning sessions in which the investigators familiarize themselves with the gang and any new information that has come to light. An investigator who is deep under cover would likely not be able to attend these sessions on a regular basis, so he or she would have to work out a system to receive information from the rest of the team.

Patience and an ability to keep cool in stressful situations are important qualities for undercover gang investigators to have. To be successful, they have to have good judgment and an ability to empathize with the people they are investigating. Empathy helps them make connections with gang members. A strong sense of integrity will prevent their empathy from getting the better of them, however, and keep them from getting too deeply and personally involved in the gang's illegal activities.

The Dangers of Discovery

One of the most dangerous aspects of going undercover to investigate gangs is the possibility of being discovered by gang members. Gang members are aware that they may be the targets of undercover investigations, and their activities frequently attract police attention. As a result, they take particular care to watch for suspicious activity from their members, particularly from newcomers and recent recruits.

Gang members may become suspicious of an undercover officer if he or she appears over-eager to meet the gang's leaders, learn the location of gang "safe houses" (where drugs, weapons, or other contraband may be stored), or attempt to arrange a meeting with a drug supplier. An investigator who asks too many direct questions about the gang's leaders or structure may also raise suspicions. Patience and an ability to listen and observe are key to gathering information without appearing too eager, curious, or inquisitive.

This Ford Police Interceptor sedan was built for undercover work. The vehicle was designed to look like a flashy street car, rather than a typical unmarked police car.

Getting the Details Right

Undercover officers have to be mindful of how they dress, drive (they can't seem to be driving with the obvious vigilance and high-alertness that officers normally display), and even where they live. An undercover officer may temporarily move out of his or her home to a location in or near the gang's territory. The undercover officer will then spend several weeks establishing his or her cover story before approaching the gang. Gang members may make attempts to check up on an undercover investigator's cover story. Often they will try to trip the investigator up by asking personal questions about his or her past.

One important element to building a believable identity is to add the right hints of truth to cover stories and assumed identities. For their cover identities, undercover investigators are often advised to keep their first names

Undercover officers watch the Maryland home of a Mara Salvatrucha gang member wanted for allegedly stabbing a fellow gang member during a fight.

and change only their last names. They may even be advised to keep the same initials. This lessens the chance of making a mistake in conversation and provides cover in case the undercover officer is recognized by someone on the street who—not knowing the officer is working undercover—calls out his or her name.

To successfully take on an undercover identity, the investigator has to know the role as well as possible. Some officers rehearse with a partner. Others write down information—including seemingly trivial details such as restaurant preferences and favorite musicians or songs —about their undercover identity and review these details every day until they are committed to memory. Investigators should also know their cover story inside and out. It may be helpful for them to include information about their own lives, such as jobs they've worked or places they know. Doing so can add a level of authenticity and makes it harder for the investigator to give himself or herself away by giving wrong or vague information. The undercover agent must not use any identifying information that would allow a gang member to determine his or her true identity and locate his or her home and family members.

Props can also provide layers of authenticity to an undercover investigator's cover story. Many investigators fill their wallets and pockets with phone numbers of made-up friends, receipts, and credit and discount cards that match their cover identity. Anything that points to the undercover investigator's real identity should be eliminated. Undercover officers should always assume that gang members could do the same sort of research on them as they have done on the gangs.

The Perils of Undercover Work

There have been cases in which patrol officers, unaware that an investigation is underway, have mistaken undercover officers for actual gang members. In May 2009, a New York Police Department officer working undercover was fatally shot by a fellow officer who reportedly saw him running down a street with his gun drawn. In the aftermath of the shooting, the department surveyed more than two hundred of its

Officers respond to the scene of a shoot-out in Houston, Texas, in which an undercover officer and a suspect were killed. The officer had been investigating the sale of stolen televisions.

undercover officers and found that thirty-three of them had been involved in gunpoint confrontations with other officers.

The strains of an undercover investigation can last long after it ends. The officer may continue to experience paranoid feelings and may find it difficult to resume his or her daily routine. Some officers suffer from post-traumatic stress disorder (PTSD) in the aftermath of an investigation. PTSD symptoms can include intrusive flashbacks and disturbing dreams, feelings of hopelessness, irritability, memory problems, trouble sleeping, feelings of guilt or shame, and being easily frightened. Many police departments have resources available to help officers deal with PTSD.

CHAPTER FOUR

LAUNCHING A CAREER IN LAW ENFORCEMENT

People are sometimes drawn to law enforcement careers for the wrong reasons. They may like the idea of putting on a uniform, carrying a gun, and ordering people around. For them, protecting the public and keeping the peace come second to fulfilling their own desire for power and authority.

Some officers who are attracted to the idea of becoming an undercover gang investigator may relish having an exciting job and helping breaking open big criminal cases. They may like the idea of pretending to be someone they are not and being seen as an edgy, "out there," roguish character by other police officers. It may not occur to them that undercover officers work long hours under extremely tense, nerve-wracking, even terrifying circumstances. They may not get to return to their homes or contact their friends and family members for months or even years on end.

Before seriously considering a career in law enforcement, a candidate should perform an honest and accurate self-assessment and make sure that he or she is motivated by the right reasons. Law enforcement officers, detectives in particular, are charged with upholding the law. According to the law enforcement Code of Ethics established by the International Association of Chiefs of Police, officers are charged with a fundamental duty to "serve mankind; to safeguard lives and property; to protect the innocent against deception, the weak against oppression or intimidation, and the peaceful against violence or disorder; and to respect the Constitutional rights of all men to liberty, equality, and justice." Candidates should be confident that they can follow this code before they become police officers.

The First Step: Becoming a Police Officer

Aspiring police officers should be aware of the challenges and drawbacks of police work. Being a police officer can be thankless work. The public often notices occasional police misconduct or scandals more than the day-to-day accomplishments of officers and the safety and security they provide to the public. The hours can be long, and most police officers and detectives do not follow a nine-to-five schedule. The stresses of police work can take a toll on the family lives of

Police training exercises test how well prospective officers can perform tasks they may face in the field. Here, a man drags a dummy during a citizen's police academy program.

officers. While salaries and wages are solid, private-sector employment would pay more for the same kind of investigative or security work.

Officers and detectives need to meet certain physical requirements. Applicants submit to a basic medical review that includes vision and hearing tests. Police departments require a certain level of physical fitness from applicants, who undergo a physical fitness test. The test often includes weight lifting, push-ups, pull-ups, sit-ups, a distance run, and an obstacle course. Some departments have a minimum age of twenty-one and a maximum age of thirty-five or forty for joining.

Prospective officers and detectives also have to go through a strict background check. Often a candidate with a past felony conviction will be disqualified from working in law enforcement. Background checks also bring up any potential problems, such as poor credit history, traffic violations, and drug use. Such a history will not necessarily disqualify a candidate from being hired, but it may raise questions about the applicant's maturity and decision-making skills. Too many such red flags may indicate a history of irresponsible, reckless, or even illegal behavior.

Education and Experience

Applicants need a minimum of a high school diploma in order to join a police force, but higher education can be beneficial for potential recruits. Some departments may consider otherwise exceptional candidates who hold a General

Equivalency Diploma (GED). Recruits who hope to become detectives should consider earning a college degree. Taking college courses can help a candidate gain specialized skills and knowledge and develop communication and critical thinking skills. College also gives students experience in talking to and interacting with people from many different kinds of backgrounds.

Earning a two-year or four-year college degree or accumulating a certain number of college credits can give an applicant an advantage in the hiring process. Many departments now require that police academy candidates earn at least a certain number of college credits. Common majors for police force applicants include criminal justice, forensic sciences, accounting, and computer science. Foreign language majors may also have an advantage in the hiring process. Some departments place an emphasis on hiring officers who are fluent in a foreign language, particularly departments in large cities with large immigrant populations.

Studying a foreign language can be particularly beneficial to candidates who want to do undercover work. Recruits who want to be undercover investigators can also separate themselves from the pack by studying theater or even psychology. These disciplines can equip recruits with the ability to assume another identity and fully inhabit it with confidence, while also teaching them how to closely observe those around them.

Some police departments may give high school students or recent graduates with an interest in law enforcement a

Officers practice giving a suspect instructions in Spanish during a language class. Many officers take classes throughout their careers to keep their skills sharp and continue to meet department requirements.

chance to learn more about the field by enrolling in a cadet program. The cadets can gain practical experience serving in a role such as "community services officer" or some other position until they become old enough to apply for the force. Requirements and duties for cadet positions vary from one department to another. For example, some departments offer paid cadet positions, while others do not. Other programs that allow civilians to participate include law enforcement explorers, police auxiliary, and police reserve officers.

Some federal, state, and local law enforcement agencies offer internships for prospective officers. Law enforcement internship programs may give participants exposure to a broad range of police duties, or they may focus on a particular subject area, such as crime analysis. These programs often require that applicants be full-time students. Volunteer opportunities may also be available through some police departments.

Work experience, even in seemingly unrelated fields, can provide skills that are useful for a career in law enforcement. A customer service job, for example, can help an applicant develop communication skills and gain experience interacting with the public. Good references from previous employers can show that the candidate has a good work ethic. Many departments give preferential hiring status to veterans and members of the National Guard and reserve branches of the military.

Police Academy

People interested in careers as police officers must attend police academy before they can begin patrolling the streets. Police academy is an intensive and rigorous program that combines practical training with classroom instruction. Recruits learn about the laws they will have to enforce while on patrol, investigative techniques, and the proper protocol for writing reports. Candidates for positions in small police departments usually attend a state or regional police academy, while large departments often operate their own academies.

Practical training includes spending time on the firing range and learning about weapons. Recruits also hit the gym, where they learn self-defense, arrest techniques, and the proper use of force. Recruits also learn driving techniques

A recruit trains in a tactics class at the Chicago police academy. The academy program lasts for six months and includes physical, practical, and academic training.

designed to cut down on the risk of auto accidents. More police officers are killed in car accidents each year than are killed by suspects.

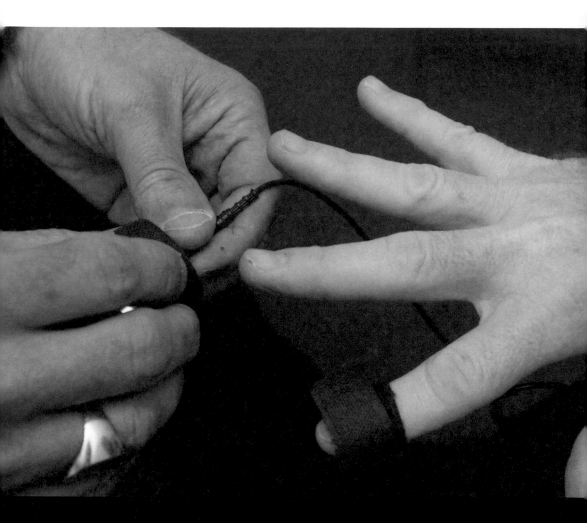

Polygraph tests help police departments screen applicants by measuring their response to questions about their past through sensors attached to their fingers.

Applying for Police Work

The first step in launching a career in law enforcement is to fill out a job application for a police department. Some

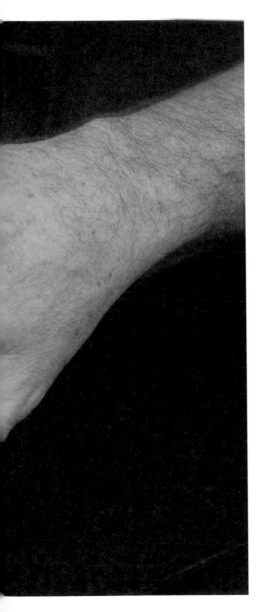

departments offer application forms online. The selection process for new recruits often begins up to six months before the start date for the next police academy class, so applicants are encouraged to start the process early. The requirements and order of the application process often vary from one department to another, but the general elements are the same. Potential recruits who do not know what to expect can usually find preparation tips and other information on the police department Web site.

The testing process for potential recruits usually consists of a physical fitness test and a written test. The physical fitness test requires applicants to demonstrate their strength, agility, endurance, and aerobic capacity. Some departments offer training tips, including recommended workout regimens, to help applicants get into shape. Applicants should know the department's physical requirements and spend months exercising regularly before taking the test. Nerves can have a negative effect on performance during the actual tests, so it is often a good idea to reach a higher physical fitness level than the department requires. Remember, though, that you should receive a checkup and consult with your doctor before beginning any new exercise program or fitness regimen.

Written aptitude tests generally include questions on reading, language usage, math, and police situations. The test may include an essay section along with multiple-choice questions. Police departments make the format of the tests available to the public so that applicants know what to study and how to prepare. Applicants should familiarize themselves with the test format, study for all the topics that might be covered, and get a good night's sleep before the test.

Many applicants worry more about meeting the physical requirements of the police department and pay less attention to preparing for the written test or oral interview. However, law enforcement experts place more importance on the oral interview portion of the process. The interview gives the applicant his or her first opportunity to make a positive impression on future supervisors and coworkers. To do well, applicants should spend time researching the department and learn as much as they can about its organizational structure, the layouts of its precincts, the names of some of the top officers, information about the community, current crime statistics and public safety issues, and the duties that are typical of an entry-level position.

To make a good impression, applicants should practice answering questions about themselves in mock interviews and prepare a closing statement to summarize their ability to do the job and their unique strengths, skills, and qualifications. Applicants should arrive early for their interview and dress appropriately. The interviewing panel will ask the candidate questions to determine if he or she has the skills, knowledge, and ability to do the job. Questions might cover hypothetical scenarios, the applicant's personal history, and his or her views on law enforcement. Applicants should consider each question carefully and avoid rushing into answers.

The police department will carry out a background check on applicants. Investigators will look at records from the candidate's personal, educational, legal, and financial history. The process may include interviews of family members, friends, and former employers and coworkers. The candidate is fingerprinted, and some departments require potential recruits to submit to a background interview. Candidates later take a polygraph exam administered by a trained poly-graph examiner. This test is used to confirm information about the candidate's background.

Candidates also submit to a psychological exam, which evaluates their psychological and emotional fitness for police work. This examination includes a written test and may require an interview with a psychologist. A medical exam confirms that the applicant is physically healthy enough for

Patrol officers may face many different kinds of situations during a shift. Here, an officer talks to a person involved in a traffic accident in Miami, Florida.

the job. Some departments also require drug testing.

Going on Patrol

Once prospective police officers successfully complete the police academy, they are hired by the department as patrol officers. New officers begin with a probation period, which usually lasts about a year. During this time, they gain experience and learn the basics of police work. They also undergo on-the-job-training or field training alongside experienced officers. For new patrol officers who want to become undercover gang investigators, this period can provide an opportunity for them to show their superiors that they have the skills needed to pull off an undercover investigation.

Patrol officers are the members of the police force who have the most direct contact with people in the community. The patrol division is often described as the backbone of the police department. Patrol officers represent the law's role in the lives of

citizens. When they are on duty, they are expected to pre-
serve the peace, prevent crime, and catch criminals. During
their shifts, they respond to dispatches from police headquarters and 911 emergency call centers, as well as direct
requests for help from the public.

The calls and service requests that patrol officers handle
can cover a wide range of situations. In addition to reports of
possible crimes, they respond to calls concerning accidents,
emergency situations, missing person reports, threats to
public safety, and disturbances of the peace. The circumstances may call for the patrol officers to issue a citation,
make an arrest, begin a preliminary investigation, or redirect
the complaint.

Patrol officers also respond to traffic accidents and
enforce parking laws and the rules of the road. They provide
crowd control at public events and can administer first aid,
if necessary. They also see to the day-to-day concerns of
the public and provide support for community crime prevention efforts.

Ambitious young patrol officers may be able to apply to
join specialized units, depending on the size of their department. In many large cities, the police department has a gang
unit that interested and qualified patrol officers can ask to
join. These specialized units often have an investigative track
that officers can follow to promotion.

In order to earn an assignment to one of these units, an
officer has to first establish himself or herself as a good and
dependable patrol officer. After proving himself or herself as

UNDERCOVER AGENTS FACE SUSPICION FROM WITHIN THE FORCE

Undercover work can occasionally have a negative impact upon a police officer's career. In her book *Art of Darkness: Ingenious Performances by Undercover Operators, Con Men, and Others*, anthropologist Sara Schneider offers advice for aspiring undercover investigators that she collected through hundreds of interviews with law enforcement personnel.

Schneider says that undercover gang investigators should always be aware of risks to their careers. Some officers and even high-level police officials may be suspicious of officers who have gone undercover for long periods of time. These officers may believe that the undercover investigator has "turned" or become a criminal during the course of the investigation. Officers who work undercover may need to meet a higher standard of excellence in all policing operations —not just undercover work—in order to overcome the taint of this stigma, distrust, and suspicion, and advance their careers.

a patrol officer over a period of time, he or she can then request an assignment to the gangs unit, get an interview, and ultimately be accepted if his or her personal and professional strengths, skills, and experience are a good fit. The interview process is not as rigorous as the steps taken to join the department initially. But candidates for an assignment to the gang unit need to be able to show that they are familiar with and qualified to carry out gang investigations.

After spending a few years on the job, a patrol officer is able to handle problematic and potentially dangerous situations with confidence. The officer will be experienced in dealing with the public as an authority figure and will be able to competently manage a crime scene. He or she will be able to write clear and accurate reports of incidents. The officer will be familiar with crime patterns in the city, particularly in his or her precinct or district. He or she will have experience in dealing with many different types of crimes. The knowledge and experience gained during this time will be invaluable once the officer earns a promotion to detective.

CHAPTER FIVE

JOINING THE FEDS

C areer possibilities in undercover gang investigations do not begin and end with local or state police departments. There are several federal law enforcement agencies that investigate criminal activity associated with gangs. These include the FBI, the ATF, and the DEA. Their investigations often focus on gangs with substantial national or even international networks, and they target weapons and narcotics traffickers. As in the 2012 investigation into the Latin Kings gang in Holland, Michigan, these agencies sometimes step in and provide assistance to local law enforcement when and if the gang and its activities are part of a broader, usually interstate or international investigation.

The hazards for these federal officers, including federal undercover agents, are similar to those faced by local and state police officers and agents, though the gangs they investigate may have a greater reputation for viciousness and brutality. These gangs include criminal organizations, such as biker gangs, and international street gang organizations, such as MS-13.

Heavily equipped FBI agents working with the Los Angeles Police Department go into an apartment building to arrest gang members on federal and state drug charges.

Federal law enforcement agencies have very rigorous standards, and the application process is time-consuming. It often takes up to a year to complete the application process.

Joining the FBI

The Federal Bureau of Investigation investigates gangs as part of its operations against organized and violent crime. FBI special agents carry out investigations that protect national security and enforce more than three hundred federal laws. Most applicants are between the ages of twenty-three and thirty-seven, though the age restriction is sometimes waived for former military personnel older than thirty-seven.

The requirements for becoming an FBI special agent are rigorous. Applicants must have a four-year degree from an accredited college or university and at least three years of professional work experience. They must be available to work in all fifty states and possess a valid driver's license.

The application process begins when the candidate submits an online application. The online application helps the FBI screen candidates. The most promising applicants are contacted and an appointment is made for them to undergo "Phase I" testing at an FBI field office. This phase of testing consists of a series of written tests. Applicants who indicated on their online application that they have special- ized experience, such as foreign language proficiency, may take additional tests in their field of expertise.

Applicants who pass the first phase of testing may then qualify for "Phase II" testing, depending on their overall qualifi- cations, their competitiveness among all applicants, and the agency's needs. This second phase of testing consists of another written test and an in-person interview with a panel of current special agents. Depending on the agency's needs and budget, candidates who pass this testing phase are given a conditional letter of appointment, which serves as an initial job offer.

Candidates who receive the conditional letter move on to the bureau's physical fitness test. The test consists of the number of sit-ups that the applicant can do in a minute, a timed 328- yard (300-meter) sprint, the number of push-ups he or she can do (without a time limit), and a timed 1.5-mile (2.4-kilometer) run. Besides the official evaluation, recruits also must perform a physical self-evaluation using the same criteria and report a passing score before undergoing Phase II testing. Candidates have three chances to pass the physical fitness evaluation, and those who don't will have to go through a waiting period before they can take the test again. Those who cannot pass the test will not be able to join a new agent training class and their conditional letters of appointment may be rescinded (cancelled).

Applicants who receive a conditional letter of appointment also have to submit the necessary paperwork for the bureau to begin a background investigation. The FBI background investigation includes a polygraph exam, credit and arrest checks, verification of the applicant's education background, and interviews with personal and business references, neigh-bors, and past employers. A medical exam follows the physical fitness test and the first stages of the background investigation. The medical exam checks for any conditions that could affect the applicant's ability to carry out the duties of a special agent. Applicants must also be able to pass hearing and vision tests.

Candidates who pass through all phases of the application process are scheduled for approximately twenty-one weeks of training at the FBI Academy in Quantico, Virginia. The academy includes time in the classroom and intensive physical training. Participants learn defensive tactics and how to use firearms, and they take part in exercises that apply what they have learned.

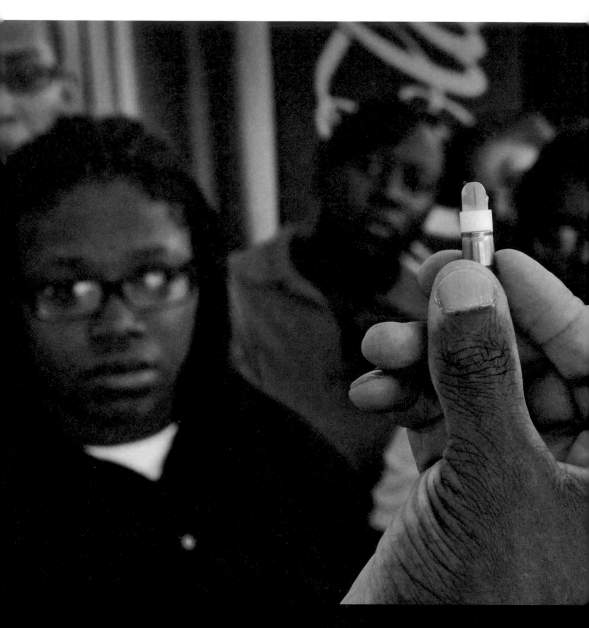

High school students touring Hogan's Alley at the FBI Training Facility in Quantico, Virginia, are shown a rubber bullet similar to those used in training exercises.

At the academy, applicants are divided into five special agent career paths: Intelligence, Counterintelligence, Counterterrorism, Criminal, and Cyber. The assignment is based on the applicant's education, prior employment, preference, skills, knowledge, and abilities. Applicants who are interested in undercover gang investigations should list "Criminal" as their preferred career path. For these applicants, a college major in criminal justice—which teaches students aspects of police work, such as interrogation techniques—can be helpful. A career background in law enforcement, participation in police cadet programs, and extensive knowledge of investigative techniques are also useful in seeking this career path.

HOGAN'S ALLEY

Both the FBI and the DEA train new recruits at the FBI Academy in Quantico, Virginia. The 547-acre campus includes three dormitory buildings, a classroom building, a dining hall, and a large gymnasium. One of the academy's most unique features is a mock town called Hogan's Alley.

Hogan's Alley was built in 1987 with the help of Hollywood set designers. It has one street and features a bank, a post office, a hotel, a laundromat, a barber shop, a pool hall, and row houses. There, trainees are taught investigative skills, self-defense tactics, and firearms skills. Actors help agents prepare for fieldwork by playing many different types of criminals, as well as innocent bystanders. The trainees plan and make arrests, investigate terrorist acts, and carry out searches for suspects. They even engage in simulated gunfights—using realistic paintball guns—under the watchful eyes of instructors. Agents sometimes joke that Hogan's Alley is the only town in the United States where a bank is robbed at least twice a week.

After completing the academy, new FBI agents are assigned to one of the bureau's fifty-six field offices. New agents can rank their desired locations, but they are ultimately assigned to a particular office based on staffing needs. Agents can be reassigned at any time but usually stay in their first assignment for two to three years. The FBI offers a competitive salary and generous benefits. It sometimes pays a relocation bonus to agents who are reassigned to an area with a high cost of living.

FBI agents assigned to the Criminal Investigative Division investigate financial crime, violent crime, organized crime, drug-related crime, public corruption, and civil rights violations. Their investigations of organized crime, drug-related crime, and violent crime include undercover investigations of street gangs.

Becoming an ATF Agent

The Bureau of Alcohol, Tobacco, Firearms, and Explosives works to prevent and investigate federal crimes involving guns, tobacco, and alcohol. The ATF's investigations into gangs are often centered on weapons trafficking or other weapons offenses, though they may also investigate the theft or illegal sale of alcohol or tobacco products by gangs. These investigations may overlap with local law enforcement or FBI investigations.

To become an ATF agent, applicants must be no younger than twenty-one and no older than thirty-six. Age limit

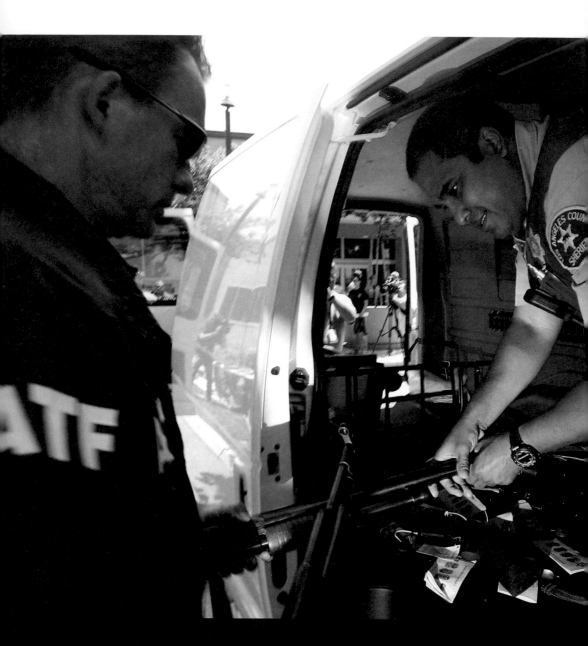

Agents with the ATF load confiscated weapons into a van following an investigation that resulted in the arrests of scores of gang members in Lakewood, California.

waivers are available for former military personnel. Prospective ATF agents must also be U.S. citizens and have a valid driver's license. The ATF requires agents to have at least a bachelor's degree—preferably in criminal justice—or at least three years of law enforcement experience. To perform the job, agents have to be legally permitted to carry a gun, meaning that certain prior felony or misdemeanor convictions can disqualify candidates from joining the ATF. Agents also have to be able to relocate at the agency's request.

As with the FBI application process, people who want to join the ATF have to fill out a questionnaire and pass a written exam and an assessment test. A physical task test is used to make sure that applicants are able to meet the rigors of training. The test consists of a 1.5-mile (2.4-km) run and how many push-ups and sit-ups the applicant can do in a minute. To pass, applicants have to meet minimum standards for each portion of the test, with only a short break between each section. The standards that must be met vary depending on the applicant's age and gender. Applicants are tested only once and are removed from the hiring process if they fail to meet any of the standards.

Applicants who successfully complete the physical test and other assessments have to appear for a field panel interview and submit a writing sample. They also have to pass a drug test, a medical exam, and a background check before they are eligible for training.

Training for ATF agents is carried out in two parts. The Criminal Investigators Training Program lasts for twelve weeks and is carried out at the Federal Law Enforcement Center in Glynco, Georgia. Each class consists of forty-eight students, half of whom are prospective ATF agents, while the other half are trainees from other federal law enforcement agencies. Candidates learn investigative techniques, concepts, and methodologies used by the ATF. Subjects covered include firearms training, physical techniques for restraining subjects and conducting searches, driving techniques, surveillance, photography, crime scene management, interviewing suspects and witnesses, and federal court procedures.

The second part of the training program is Special Agent Basic Training. It lasts for approximately fifteen weeks and takes place at the Federal Law Enforcement Center. Each class includes twenty-four prospective agents and is designed to teach recruits the basic skills that they will need as ATF agents. Classroom time includes instruction in firearms technology, trafficking and trafficking regulations, arson and arson regulations, explosives and explosives regulations, legal issues, field operations, and undercover regulations. How to write reports, conduct interviews, and seize property is also covered. Trainees learn about legal issues such as constitutional protections against unreasonable searches and seizures, federal law, and constitutional law. Recruits must take seven exams during the training program and pass each of them with at least an 80 percent.

Recruits receive approximately one hundred hours of firearms training designed to familiarize them with handguns, rifles, and shotguns. Trainees are instructed in tactical marksmanship, tactical marksmanship on the move, low light tactical shooting, flying on a commercial plane with a concealed weapon, and handling concealed weapons. In order to become full-fledged agents, trainees must score at least 80 percent on two consecutive handgun marksmanship tests.

Arson and explosives training gives academy students a basic foundation for investigating the criminal misuse of

Agents prepare to enter a vacant apartment building that was bombed as part of a training exercise. The exercise was designed to help agents sharpen their investigation techniques.

explosives and fire. Trainees learn how to identify types of explosives, process a bomb scene, and gather evidence. They also receive hands-on instruction in handling explosives.

Tactical training teaches prospective agents how to take control of dangerous situations in which they face armed suspects. As part of their tactical training, trainees are required to successfully complete a final assessment called the Final Tactical Practical. This test includes a half-mile (0.8-km) run in full tactical gear, a "shoot/no shoot" exercise, a demonstration of proper use of force, and a simulated agent extraction in which trainees have to drag a 100-pound (45-kilogram) dummy 25 yards (23 m). Trainees also participate in approximately fifty-six hours of physical training and seventy-two hours of close-quarter countermeasures training, which includes self-defense and handcuffing techniques.

Once they graduate from their training, the new agents can be assigned to any ATF office in the United States or to any U.S. territory. ATF agents routinely endure dangerous situations, irregular hours, and extensive travel. Agents receive benefits and a base pay rate, plus additional pay based on the location of their assignment. They also can receive a cash award if they use a foreign language in the course of carrying out their duties.

A DEA agent unloads marijuana that was seized during a drug bust in Fresno, California. Some of the drugs had been packed and were ready to be shipped to buyers.

Joining the DEA

The mission of the Drug Enforcement Administration is to combat illegal drug smuggling and drug use in the United States. The agency investigates and builds cases against drug traffickers, gangs, and individuals who sell, profit from, and commit acts of violence and intimidation in connection with illegal drugs. The DEA makes extensive use of surveillance techniques and undercover operations to expose drug-related crimes.

The age and citizenship requirements for becoming a DEA agent are the same as those for joining the ATF and the FBI. Applicants need to have at least a bachelor's degree in criminal justice. People who want to become DEA agents must meet vision and hearing requirements and be able to lift at least 45 pounds (20 kg). If they meet the basic requirements, they are cleared to contact a DEA field office to schedule an orientation session, during which they will fill out an application. Prospective agents whose applications are accepted must pass drug tests, a polygraph test, a background check, a psychological assessment, a medical exam, a witness assessment, and a physical task test.

Applicants who pass these tests advance to the DEA Training Academy in Quantico, Virginia. Agent basic training lasts for eighteen weeks. Trainees live at the academy for the duration of their training. Classes usually have between forty and fifty prospective agents, with an average age of thirty years. About 60 percent of the trainees have previous law enforcement experience.

The training program is split between time in the classroom and physical training. Classroom sessions cover report writing, the law, automated information systems, drug recognition, ethics, and leadership. Prospective agents are also required to undergo a rigorous 84-hour physical training course and 122 hours of firearms training. In order to graduate, trainees have to carry an 80 percent average on academic examinations, pass the firearms qualification test, pass physical task tests, and demonstrate leadership and sound decision-making skills in high-pressure scenarios. Graduates are sworn in as DEA special agents and assigned to DEA field offices across the United States.

GLOSSARY

administrative Pertaining to management of the daily operations of an organization.

affiliation One's connection with a group or organization.

alleged Declared to be true, but not proven.

apprehend To arrest.

cadet A student training to become a law enforcement officer.

convict To find someone guilty of committing a crime.

crime lab A laboratory in which physical evidence from criminal cases is examined and analyzed.

criminologist One who studies crime, criminals, and punishments.

defendant Someone who has been accused of committing a crime.

drug trafficking The crime of dealing (including selling and transporting) in illegal drugs.

faction A small group within a larger group, often with different ideas or opinions from the rest.

felony A serious crime; specifically, a federal crime for which the punishment may range from imprisonment for more than a year to life imprisonment or death by execution.

forensic science The application of scientific knowledge to legal problems, matters, or questions.

gang A group of people working together for illegal or antisocial ends.

graffiti Words or pictures drawn in public places, often without permission.

informant Someone who secretly gives information about others to the police or to some other authority.

narcotics A class of substances that dull the senses and that, when used in large quantities over time, can be addictive.

personnel The people employed at an organization or place of work.

probation The trial process or period in which a person's fitness for employment in a certain job is tested.

prosecutor The attorney who pursues legal action against someone or something in court on behalf of the government.

surveillance Close observation or monitoring, often of a person or group under suspicion.

suspect Someone who is believed to have committed a crime.

undercover Acting or carried out in secret and with an assumed or disguised identity.

warrant An authorization issued by a judge, such as to search for evidence or make an arrest.

witness Someone who has seen or can give firsthand evidence of a crime.

FOR MORE INFORMATION

Bureau of Alcohol, Tobacco, Firearms, and Explosives (ATF)
Office of Public and Governmental Affairs
99 New York Avenue NE, Room 5S 144
Washington, DC 20226
(800) 800-3855
Web site: http://www.atf.gov
The ATF enforces federal laws concerning alcohol and
    tobacco products, firearms, explosives, and arson.

Canadian Police Association (CPA)
141 Catherine Street, Suite 100
Ottawa, ON K2P 1C3
Canada
(613) 231-4168
Web site: http://www.cpa-acp.ca
The Canadian Police Association is the national organization
    of Canadian police personnel.

Drug Enforcement Administration (DEA)
8701 Morrissette Drive
Springfield, VA 22152
(202) 307-1000
Web site: http://www.justice.gov/dea
The DEA is the federal agency responsible for enforcing laws
    and regulations governing narcotics and controlled
    substances.

Federal Bureau of Investigation (FBI)
FBI Headquarters
935 Pennsylvania Avenue NW
Washington, DC 20535-0001

(202) 324-3000

Web site: http://www.fbi.gov

The Federal Bureau of Investigation is the agency charged
with investigating a broad range of federal crimes.

International Association of Chiefs of Police (IAC)

515 North Washington Street

Alexandria, VA 22314

(703) 836-6767

Web site: http://www.theiacp.org

The International Association of Chiefs of Police is the organization of police executives dedicated to providing global
leadership in policing.

International Association of Undercover Officers

148 Banks Drive

Brunswick, GA 31523

(800) 876-5943

Web site: http://www.undercover.org

The International Association of Undercover Officers pro-
motes safety and professionalism among undercover
officers.

International Association of Women Police (IAWP)

12600 Kavanaugh Lane

Bowie, MD 20715

(301) 464-1402

Web site: http://www.iawp.org

The International Association of Women Police aims to
strengthen, unite, and raise the profile of women in
criminal justice.

National Alliance of Gang Investigators' Associations

P.O. Box 782

Elkhorn, NE 68022

(402) 510-8581

Web site: http://www.nagia.org/index.asp

The National Alliance of Gang Investigators Associations (NAGIA) is a cooperative organization representing twenty state and regional gang investigators associations with over twenty thousand members. It provides for leadership in developing and recommending strategies to prevent and control gang crime, administer professional training, and assist criminal justice professionals and the public in identifying and tracking gangs, gang members, and gang crime around the world.

National Gang Center

Institute for Intergovernmental Research

P.O. Box 12729

Tallahassee, FL 32317

(850) 385-0600

Web site: http://www.nationalgangcenter.gov

The National Gang Center is the U.S. Department of Justice's clearinghouse of public information about gangs.

Office of Juvenile Justice and Delinquency Prevention

810 Seventh Street NW

Washington, DC 20531

(202) 307–5911

Web site: http://www.ojjdp.gov/index.html

The Office of Juvenile Justice and Delinquency Prevention (OJJDP) provides national leadership, coordination, and resources to prevent and respond to juvenile delinquency and victimization. OJJDP supports states and communities in their efforts to develop and implement effective and coordinated prevention and intervention programs and to improve the juvenile justice system so that it protects public safety, holds offenders accountable, and provides treatment and rehabilitative services tailored to the needs of juveniles and their families.

Royal Canadian Mounted Police (RCMP)
RCMP National Headquarters
73 Leikin Drive
Ottawa, ON K1A 0R2
Canada
(613) 993-7267
Web site: http://www.rcmp-grc.gc.ca
The Royal Canadian Mounted Police is Canada's national police service.

U.S. Department of Justice (DOJ)
950 Pennsylvania Avenue NW
Washington, DC 20530-0001
(202) 514-2000
Web site: http://www.justice.gov
The U.S. Department of Justice is the nation's primary federal criminal investigation and enforcement agency.

Web Sites

Due to the changing nature of Internet links, Rosen Publishing has developed an online list of Web sites related to the subject of this book. This site is updated regularly. Please use this link to access the list:

http://www.rosenlinks.com/LAW/Gang

FOR FURTHER READING

Chambliss, William J. *Police and Law Enforcement.* Thousand Oaks, CA: Sage, 2011.

Dempsey, John S., and Linda S. Forst. *An Introduction to Policing.* 6th ed. Clifton Park, NY: Delmar Cengage Learning, 2011.

Foster, Raymond E., and Tracey Vasil Biscontini. *Police Officer Exam for Dummies.* Hoboken, NJ: Wiley Publishing, 2011.

Gilbert. James N. *Criminal Investigation.* 8th ed. Boston, MA: Prentice Hall, 2009.

Harr, J. Scott, and Kären M. Hess. *Careers in Criminal Justice and Related Fields: From Internship to Promotion.* 6th ed. Belmont, CA: Wadsworth Publishing, 2009.

Hess, Kären M., and Christine Hess Orthmann. *Management and Supervision in Law Enforcement.* 6th ed. Clifton Park, NY: Delmar Cengage Learning, 2011.

Klein, Malcolm W., and Cheryl L. Maxson. *Street Gang Patterns and Policies.* New York, NY: Oxford University Press, 2010.

Learning Express Editors. *Becoming a Police Officer.* New York, NY: LearningExpress, 2009.

Regoli, Robert, John Hewitt, and Matt DeLis. *Delinquency in Society.* 8th ed. Burlington, MA: Jones and Bartlett Publishers, 2009.

Roberts, Walter. *Biker Gangs.* Newport, RI: RW Press, 2012.

Rogers, June Werdlow. *Now Hiring: Criminal Justice Professionals.* Brule, WI: Cable Publishing, 2011.

Saferstein, Richard. *Forensic Science: From the Crime Scene to the Crime Lab.* 2nd ed. Boston, MA, Prentice Hall, 2012.

Samaha, Joel. *Criminal Procedure*. 8th ed. Belmont, CA: Wadsworth Publishing, 2011.

Schmalleger, Frank. *Criminal Justice Today: An Introductory Text for the 21st Century*. 11th ed. Boston, MA: Prentice Hall, 2010.

Schmalleger, Frank, and John L. Worrall. *Policing Today*. Boston, MA: Prentice Hall, 2009.

Schroeder, Donald J., and Frank A. Lombardo. *Police Officer Exam*. 8th ed. Hauppauge, NY: Barron's, 2009.

Siegel, Larry J., and John L. Worrall. *Introduction to Criminal Justice*. 13th ed. Belmont, CA: Wadsworth Publishing, 2011.

Swanson, Charles, et. al. *Criminal Investigation*. 11th ed. New York, NY: McGraw-Hill, 2011.

Valdez, Al. *Gangs: A Guide to Understanding Street Gangs*. 5th ed. San Clemente, CA: LawTech Publishing, 2009.

Wallace, Harvey, and Cliff Roberson. *Principles of Criminal Law*. 5th ed. Boston, MA: Prentice Hall, 2011.

BIBLIOGRAPHY

Agar, John. "Prosecutor: Holland Latin Kings Face Racketeering Probe, Gang Member Busted Outside of Bar." *Grand Rapids Press*, December 4, 2012. Retrieved December 2012 (http://www.mlive.com/news/grand-rapids/index.ssf/2012/12/prosecutor_holland_latin_kings.html).

Agar, John. "U.S. Attorney Patrick Miles Says Cooperation of Police Agencies Led to Holland Latin King Indictments." *Grand Rapids Press*, February 21, 2013. Retrieved February 2013 (http://www.mlive.com/news/grand-rapids/index.ssf/2013/02/us_attorney_patrick_miles_says.html).

Caine, Alex. *Befriend and Betray: Infiltrating the Hells Angels, Bandidos, and Other Criminal Brotherhoods*. New York, NY: Thomas Dunne Books, 2008.

Carr, Patrick J. *Clean Streets: Containing Crime, Maintaining Order, and Building Community Activism*. New York, NY: New York University Press, 2005.

Chicago Crime Commission. *The Chicago Crime Commission Gang Book*. Chicago, IL: Chicago Crime Commission, 2012.

Delattre, Edwin. *Character and Cops: Ethics in Policing*. 3rd ed. Washington, DC: The AEI Press, 1996.

Dobyns, Jay, and Nils Johnson-Shelton. *No Angel: My Harrowing Undercover Journey to the Inner Circle of the Hells Angels*. New York, NY: Crown Publishers, 2009.

Douglas, John E. *John Douglas's Guide to Landing a Career in Law Enforcement*. New York, NY: McGraw-Hill, 2005.

Douglas, John E. *John Douglas's Guide to the Police Officer Exams: Practical Tools to Help You Score Higher*. 4th ed. New York, NY: Kaplan Publishing, 2011.

Echaore-McDavid, Susan. *Career Opportunities in Law Enforcement, Security, and Protective Services.* 2nd ed. New York, NY: Checkmark Books, 2006.

Goetz, Kristina. "Undercover Police Work in Memphis Neighborhoods Ravaged by Drugs." *Commercial-Appeal*, November 20, 2009. Retrieved January 2013 (http://www.commercialappeal.com/news/2009/nov/20/under-cover-for-addicts-streets-are-a-buyers-in).

Grant, Susan. "Going Undercover." Officer.com, October 2, 2007. Retrieved February 2013 (http://www.officer.com/article/10249412/going-undercover).

Gumbrecht, Jamie. "ICP: Hate Us, Don't Hate the Fans." CNN, August 17, 2012. Retrieved February 2013 (http://www.cnn.com/2012/08/16/showbiz/icp-juggalo-fbi-lawsuit).

Howell, James C., and John P. Moore. "History of Street Gangs in the United States." *National Gang Center Bulletin*, May 2010. Retrieved January 2013 (http://www.nationalgangcenter.gov/Content/Documents/History-of-Street-Gangs.pdf).

Joh, Elizabeth E. "Breaking the Law to Enforce It: Undercover Police Participation in Crime." *Stanford Law Review*, February 24, 2010. Retrieved January 2013 (http://legalworkshop.org/2010/02/24/breaking-the-law-to-enforce-it-undercover-police-participation-in-crime).

Johnson, Carrie. "Feds Peel Back Chrome on Motorcycle Gangs." NPR, July 29, 2010. Retrieved December 2012 (http://www.npr.org/templates/story/story.php?storyId=128826377).

Kelling, George L., and Catherine M. Coles. *Fixing Broken Windows: Restoring Order and Reducing Crime in Our Communities.* New York, NY: Martin Kessler Books, 1996.

Kovaleski, Serge F. "Two Officers' Paths to a Fatal Encounter in Harlem." *New York Times*, May 29, 2009. Retrieved January 2013 (http://www.nytimes.com/2009/05/30 /nyregion/30officers.html?pagewanted=all&_r=0).

Lambert, Stephen, and Debra Regan. *Great Jobs for Criminal Justice Majors*. 2nd ed. New York, NY: McGraw-Hill, 2007.

Meisner, Jason. "Latin Kings Stung by Undercover Agent." *Chicago Tribune*, September 14, 2012. Retrieved January 2012 (http://articles.chicagotribune.com /2012-09-14/news/ct-met-latin-king-roundup-20120914_1_latin-kings-gang-members-undercover-agent).

Ortmeier, P. J. *Introduction to Law Enforcement and Criminal Justice*. 2nd ed. Upper Saddle River, NJ: Pearson Education, 2006.

Queen, William. *Under and Alone: The True Story of the Undercover Agent Who Infiltrated America's Most Violent Outlaw Motorcycle Gang*. New York, NY: Random House, 2005.

Schmidt, Michael S. "Report Highlights Special Risk of Undercover Police Work." *New York Times*, November 30, 2009. Retrieved January 2013 (http://www.nytimes. com/2009/12/01/nyregion/01undercover.html?_r=0).

Schneider, Sara K. *Art of Darkness: Ingenious Performances by Undercover Operators, Con Men, and Others*. Chicago, IL: Cuneiform Books, 2008.

Skogan, Wesley G. *Police and Community in Chicago: A Tale of Three Cities*. New York, NY: Oxford University Press, 2006.

VanCook, Jerry. *Going Undercover: Secrets and Sound Advice for the Undercover Officer*. Boulder, CO: Paladin Press, 1996.

Weisel, Deborah Lamm, and Tara O'Connor Shelley. "Specialized Gang Units: Form and Function in

Community Policing, Final Report." National Criminal
Justice Reference Service, October 2004. Retrieved
December 2012 (https://www.ncjrs.gov/App/Publications
/abstract.aspx?ID=207204).

INDEX

A

administrative staff members, 26
arrests, staged, 42, 44
Art of Darkness: Ingenious Performances by Undercover Operators, Con Men, and Others, 75
Aryan Brotherhood, 35

B

background checks, 62, 71, 81, 88, 94
Bandidos, 33
Bloods, 31
Bureau of Alcohol, Tobacco, Firearms, and Explosives (ATF), 50, 77, 94
  becoming an ATF agent, 85–92

C

cadet programs, 65
civilian positions in gang units, 25–26
coercion, 12
college/college degrees, 63, 80, 87
colors, gang, 30, 36, 51
committing crimes, undercover investigators and, 7–8, 16, 44, 50
community leaders, 13

cover stories to infiltrate gangs, 40, 46, 54–57
crime lab scientists, 25
Criminal Investigative Division of the FBI, 85
criminologists, 13
Crips, 31

D

dangers of undercover gang investigation, 7–8, 16, 43, 44–45, 51–52, 57–58
DEA Training Academy, 94–95
discovery, dangers of, 51–52
dispatchers, 26
district attorneys, 12, 22–25
Drug Enforcement Administration (DEA), 27, 77, 84
  joining the, 94–95
drug testing, 73, 88, 94

E

equipment technicians, 19–21
evidence technicians, 19
exams/tests
  drug, 73, 88, 94
  medical, 71–73, 81, 88, 94
  physical, 62, 69, 80–81, 87–88, 94
  polygraph, 71, 81, 94
  psychological, 71, 94

About the Author

Jason Porterfield is a writer and journalist living in Chicago, Illinois, where he has covered crime and public safety issues for multiple publications. He has written more than twenty young adult books for Rosen Publishing, including *The Third Amendment: The Right to Privacy in the Home*, *Freedom of Speech or Defamation? Expressing Yourself on the Web*, and *Tattoos and Secret Societies*.

Photo Credits